Get Growing!

How
the Earth
Feeds Us

By Candace Savage
Illustrated by Gary Clement

**earth
care
books**

FIREFLY BOOKS

Text copyright © 1991 by Candace Savage
Illustrations copyright © 1991 by Gary Clement

First published in Canada by
Douglas & McIntyre Ltd.

Published in the United States by
Firefly Books (U.S.) Inc.
P.O. Box 1325
Ellicott Station
Buffalo, New York 14205

Canadian Cataloguing in Publication Data

Savage, Candace, 1949-
    Get growing!

(Earthcare books)
Includes index.
ISBN 0-920668-95-X

1. Agricultural conservation — Juvenile literature.
2. Agricultural ecology — Juvenile literature.
3. Agricultural — Juvenile literature.
4. Agricultural pollution — Juvenile literature.
I. Clement, Gary.   II. Title.   III. Series.

S604.5.S38 1991   j333.76'16   C91-094275-7

Special thanks to Dr. Darwin Anderson and Dr. John Stewart, College of Agriculture, University of Saskatchewan; Dr. Ewen Coxworth, Saskatchewan Research Council; and Dr. Bruno Schiefer, Toxicology Research Centre, University of Saskatchewan.

Design by Michael Solomon
Printed and bound in Hong Kong

Contents

CHAPTER 1
Who's That on Your Plate?

Picture yourself at the table surrounded by piles of food—platters, jugs, bowls and trays of beautiful, beckoning food. Ice cream and pizzas and salty chips. Hamburgers, melons, banana splits. It makes a person feel happy just to think of it.

Food matters, especially to kids. And so it should. The fact is that nothing is more important. Nothing at all. If you have enough food and the right kinds, you grow fast and don't get sick very often. You can learn and think, and are likely to live long enough to be a grandparent.

If you don't get enough to eat, you grow slowly and are sick a lot. You can't concentrate or learn very well, and you will probably die when you're still quite young.

That's pretty basic, isn't it?

If you have three meals a day and live for seventy years, you will eat 76,650 plates of food—and that's not counting snacks!

Food matters. So why do you suppose that we seldom think about it? I mean, *really think*. For example, when was the last time you actually looked at your breakfast cereal or studied your cheese sandwich? Do those corn flakes come from corn plants? Does the sugar you sprinkle into the bowl grow somewhere, or is it made in factories? And what about the cheese slices? How are they made? Do they come from near your home or from far away? How do they get to you?

Make a list of your own questions—anything at all. What are marshmallows made of? Why can't people eat sand? Is the soil hurt when we use it to grow crops? Don't worry if some of your ideas seem a little odd. "Dumb" questions are often the most important of all.

Why Dinner Plates Are Round

For example, have you ever wondered why dinner plates are round? Why aren't they squares, so they'd fit in the cupboard better, or triangles or hexagons, for variety?

I think I know why. Dinner plates are round because a circle shape is beautiful and whole. There are no bumps or gaps, no sharp corners, no beginnings and no ends. The rim goes round and round.

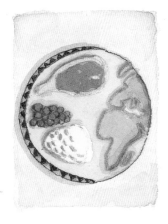

Nature is like that, too. Things go round and round. Rain falls from the clouds onto the ocean and land. When the sun shines, water is drawn back into the sky, forms new clouds and falls to the earth again. Round and round it goes.

When a tree turns green in the spring, its roots take what it needs from the soil so that the leaves can grow. When the leaves fall to the ground, they rot and give nutrients back to the soil, so the tree can grow some more. Nothing is wasted.

Round and round it goes. Plants take in water from the soil and a gas called carbon dioxide from the air, zap them with sunlight and make food for themselves and for animals like us. As they do this, plants give off another gas called oxygen. You and I breathe in this oxygen and eat the food that was made by plants. As we do this, we breathe carbon dioxide into the air. Plants take in this carbon dioxide . . . and so it goes.

When we have digested our food, our bodies release the parts that we cannot use. We call this human waste—urine and excrement—and flush it away as fast as we can. But there is no waste in

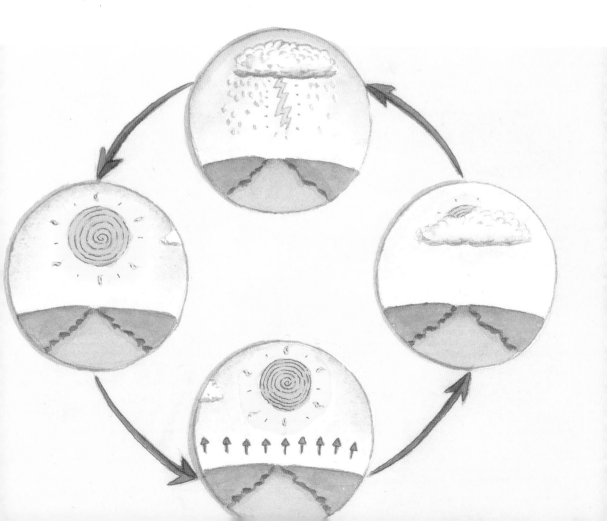

Plants cannot live without sunshine, clear air, clean water and healthy soil. Can you?

the cycles of the Earth. Our waste, and our bodies when we die, belong to the soil. They provide food for tiny creatures in the dirt, which turn them into nutrients for plants.

More plants, to feed more people and animals, whose wastes feed more plants, which feed the next generation of people and animals. Round and round we go.

The Earth always thinks in circles. It is these natural cycles—of rain and soil, of sunshine, air, insects, birds, animals and plants—that keep us alive.

Food is about cycles. And that, I think, explains why dinner plates are round.

Why Do We Have to Eat Anyway?

People are made out of ordinary, non-living stuff, or "chemicals"—the same kinds of materials that make up rocks, water and air. The main difference is that the chemicals in our bodies are put together in special ways. Although we can make some of these special chemicals, there are many that we cannot produce for ourselves.

But plants can. They can take simple chemicals from the air and soil and turn them into exactly what we need to survive.

Most of our food comes directly from plants: vegetables, fruits, nuts, seeds, beans, flours, grains and cereals. Even treats like chocolate (from the cacao tree) and sugar (from sugar cane and sugar beets) are plant foods. The rest of our diet comes mainly from animals—cows, pigs, goats, sheep, chickens and turkeys—that have eaten plants.

Food is a gift to us from the other creatures of the Earth.

*It's time to change
Our stuck-up attitude.
Hug a plant!
Let's show some
gratitude.*

Delicious Definitions
EARTH WORDS

Agriculture: Farming, a way of using the Earth so that it produces more food for us to eat.

Chemicals: The building blocks from which everything in the universe is made.

Cycle: A process in which materials are used over and over again.

Food: Plants and animals we eat because they give us the special chemicals we need and cannot make for ourselves.

Nutrient: A simple chemical that a plant or animal needs in order to grow.

Resource: Something we can use to make life better for ourselves. For example, soil is one of the resources we use to grow food.

First, get some seeds for a chocolate cake tree . . . (Wouldn't it be fun if you could?) Even though we can't grow cakes, farmers do grow most of the ingredients from which cakes are made. Like the rest of our food, chocolate cake comes from plants and from animals that eat plants, and all of them are raised on farms.

Some foods, like eggs, come straight from the farm to our plates.

Deluxe Cocoa Cake
125 mL (1/2 cup) butter
250 mL (1 cup) sugar
2 eggs
5 mL (1 tsp) vanilla
250 mL (1 cup) cocoa
375 mL (1 1/2 cups) flour
15 mL (1 tbsp) baking powder
250 mL (1 cup) milk

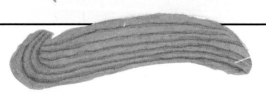

CHOCOLATE CAKE

Others, like wheat, sugar cane, cream and cacao beans, make longer trips. Before they get to us, they are taken to mills, dairies, refineries or factories and turned into "processed" foods such as flour, sugar, butter and cocoa. It's hard to believe that they came from the land, but they did. In the case of food, all roads lead back to a farm.

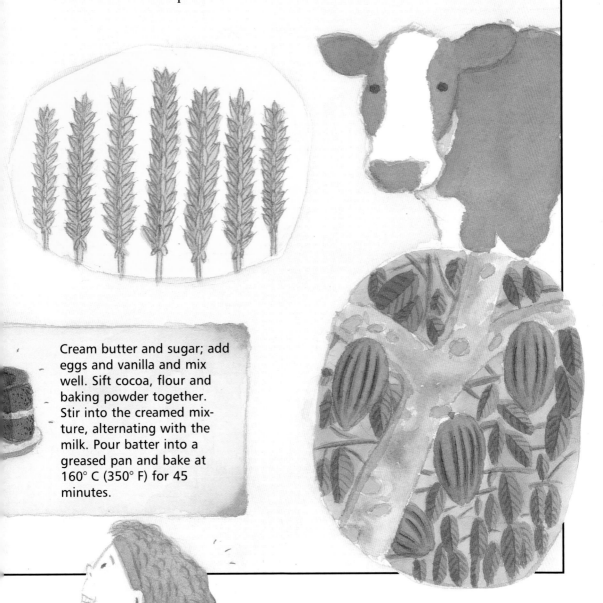

Cream butter and sugar; add eggs and vanilla and mix well. Sift cocoa, flour and baking powder together. Stir into the creamed mixture, alternating with the milk. Pour batter into a greased pan and bake at 160° C (350° F) for 45 minutes.

A Brief History of the Human Race

In the beginning, and for millions of years, people were fed directly by the natural goodness of the Earth. They gathered berries, nuts and seeds from the fields; caught fish and other water creatures in the rivers, lakes and seas; they hunted for grouse, ducks, sheep, deer, bison and antelope.

Then, just a few thousand years ago, came the biggest change in human history, much bigger than the invention of television or putting people on the moon. People invented farming. To this day, most of what we eat is grown on farms.

Farming, or agriculture, is a way of using the Earth so that it grows more of the plants and animals that people like to eat (and less of all the other things it grows naturally). Take wheat, for example. Before farming began, wheat was just an ordinary wild grass that grew in crowded meadows with many other kinds of plants. There it had to compete for a share of the soil, sun and rain that it needed to grow. Each year, a wild wheat plant could only produce a thimbleful of seeds. They were better to eat than most, but there were not very many of them.

Then somebody had a crazy thought. What would happen if you dug the meadow up, pulled out the other plants, and seeded the plot to wheat? Just wheat. If the wheat had the sun, soil and rain to itself, if you watered, weeded and killed the insects that ate its leaves, would it produce more seeds for people to eat? The answer turned out to be "yes."

"Producing more food" is what farming is all about. A successful farm grows more of the few kinds of plants and animals that people have chosen to eat. More human foods—but less of other

things. More land planted to wheat, for example, means less space for wild plants. Fewer kinds of wild plants mean fewer of the insects that use the plants for food and shelter. Fewer kinds of insects means fewer insect-eating birds and fewer bird-eating animals. One loss leads to the next.

If we farm wisely, always keeping in mind the way the Earth works, these losses can be small. But if we are greedy or wrong-headed, the losses become great. Agriculture is powerful, but it can also be dangerous.

The Grocery Machine

Some people don't like to think about the round-about cycles of the Earth, which give us our food. They want to think in straight lines. From A to Z. Start to finish. Producer to consumer. Raw material to finished goods. They forget that every ending is a new beginning.

When we try to "think straight" about growing food, we end up treating the Earth as if it were a factory. We act as if it were a huge grocery-making machine, which only exists to give us things to eat. We forget about all the other creatures that are also fed by the Earth and that, indirectly, may help to feed us, too. We forget about the people who will come after us, who will also need to eat. We

Don't Delay. Get Growing Today!

The best way to learn about food is to grow some for yourself. All you need is a window, a pot of dirt and a few seeds. Lettuce, radishes, parsley, cherry tomatoes and small cucumbers are all happy to grow in window boxes or pots. If your family has a garden, why not ask to have a corner for yourself? Better yet, share it with a friend. Cultivate your friendship while your garden grows.

completely forget that we have to give something back to the Earth so that it can continue to work. All we care about is how much we can get for ourselves right now.

For the past few lifetimes, the straight-thinkers have been in charge of growing food. In some ways they have made things run very well indeed. They have produced amazing, big, delicious heaps of food. In Europe and North America, we are up to our ears in yummy things to eat.

What a lot of food we'd munch If all five billion came to lunch!

These days, a regular kid from a regular house on a regular street anywhere in Canada, the United States, western Europe or Australia eats better than the richest king or queen in all of history.

There are now more than 5,000,000,000 people on planet Earth. Five *billion*, and the number doubles every forty years. By the year 2000, there will be six billion of us, or more. If we climbed on one another's shoulders, we would form a tower more than halfway to the Sun. If we stood side by side, the line would go around the Earth ten times. Any way you put it, there are a lot of us. Still, for the moment, our farms are producing just about enough to feed everyone (though many people do not get their share).

LOOK WHO'S COME FOR LUNCH!

Here is an easy (and slightly messy) way to see who you're eating for lunch. All you need are toothpicks, paper, crayons or colored pencils, tape, scissors and a ruler.

- First, use a ruler and pencil to divide the paper into small rectangles.
- Make little flags by cutting out the rectangles and taping each one to the wide end of a toothpick. Draw food plants on some of them—vegetables, fruits and grains. Draw animals on the rest—perhaps chickens, cows and pigs.
- At mealtime, take your flags to the table with you. Look at what is on your plate. Think about one food at a time. If it came from plants, put a plant flag in it. If it came from animals, choose an animal flag.

(If it came from animals that *ate* plants, you might want to put in both kinds of flags.)

Some foods are mixtures of ingredients that come from both plants and animals. Bread, for example, contains flour from plants and milk and eggs from animals. Put both kinds of flags into a food like this.

- If you don't know where something comes from, ask an adult for help. If the food came in a box, bag, jar or tin, you'll probably find hints in the list of ingredients that is printed on the package.
- If you are eating something runny, like soup, try sticking the flags into small pieces of toast and floating them on top. Be ready to grab them when they start to sink!

It sounds as though our way of growing food is a huge success. So what's the problem? The problem is that we are taking goodness out of the Earth—vast amounts of food—and not putting enough goodness back. Slowly but surely, we are turning the soil to sand in many parts of the world. We are polluting the water and air with harmful farm chemicals, which we cannot take out again. We are losing the natural beauty of the Earth—forests, meadows, butterflies and birds—because we want everything for ourselves, and fast!

At the end of our straight-line process, we have piles of food, but we have less of everything else, including the things we will one day need to grow food for you, me and the other 5,999,999,998 people with whom we will soon share the Earth.

If we leave less for the future, *less* is what we will get.

B E C O M E   A   W A S T E   W A T C H E R

"Clean up your plate. Lots of children would be glad to have what you're throwing out." Do your parents ever say that? When I was a kid, mine said it all the time, and I never figured out exactly what they meant. How did it help a hungry child if I ate all my food? (Answer: It didn't, of course.) But at the same time, I knew that what my parents were saying made some kind of sense.

I think I know why now. When we throw food away, we are throwing away some of the goodness of the Earth. We are throwing out the clean air that was polluted by exhaust from farm tractors and trucks. We are wasting clean water that was dirtied with farm chemicals and soil that became worn out because we took bad care of it. We are making it harder to produce enough food to keep everyone fed. Wasting food does cause hunger.

So learn to love leftovers. Demand doggy bags. Don't pile more on your plate than you're likely to eat. Patrol the back corners of your fridge, so food won't get lost there and rot. By refusing to waste food, you are helping to protect the growing power of Earth. You are helping to make sure that people can be fed.

WHO EATS AND WHO DOES NOT

Large numbers can be hard to understand. For example, if someone asked you to imagine 500 million people, your mind would likely blur. Five hundred million people would fill 10,000 huge football stadiums. Standing side by side, they would make a ring clear around the equator.

Five hundred million is the number of people who get far less than they need to eat. Every year, 40 million people die of hunger and hunger-caused sicknesses. That's like three jumbo jets full each day.

Most hungry people live in Latin America, Africa and Asia, but there is hunger in every part of the world, even in the rich countries of Australia, Europe and North America. The people who go hungry are poor.

They do not have enough land to grow food for themselves; they do not have money to buy what they need to eat.

People used to think that the way to end hunger was just to produce more food. So, not too long before you were born, scientists developed new kinds of wheat and rice that grew more grain than the old-fashioned sorts. They figured out how to use special chemicals, called fertilizers and pesticides, to make the new crops produce even more. More and more food, at a lower and lower cost. For the first time in history, the amount of food on Earth increased faster than the number of mouths waiting to be fed.

But this miracle did not solve all our problems. It did not help people who were too poor to buy the fancy seeds and farm chemicals. And, because it was based on straight-thinking, it did not help us take care of the soil, water, air and other resources that we need to feed ourselves.

If we want to end hunger, we need to learn better ways of growing our food—simpler, more natural, cheaper ways that do not harm the Earth. Today, farmers, scientists and other people around the world are working to do just that, and you can help. Read on!

CHAPTER 2

Feeding Our Friends in the Soil

When was the last time you said "thank you" to the dirt? Sounds crazy, doesn't it, saying thanks to a handful of boring, dead dust?

But the soil is neither boring, nor dead. Without it, you would starve to death. Every bite you eat—every meat loaf, soft drink, salad or pretzel—originally came from the soil. Either it started out as a plant, rooted in the earth, or as an animal that ate plants that were rooted there. And the soil around those roots did more than hold the plants in place. It was alive: it worked to help the plants grow.

A world of strange, interesting creatures live in the thin, top layer of soil. You can find them everywhere—in a plant pot, garden or park. When you run across the grass, your feet fly over them and their dark, damp universe.

In a handful of healthy dirt, there are millions of these little animals and plants. Most are so small that they can only be seen through a microscope. But you'll be able to watch the rest, walking and wriggling amongst the crumbs of soil. Beetles with wings and beetles without, centipedes, millipedes, ants, mites (tiny spiders), snails, grubs, short roundworms, fat earthworms—thousands of different sorts. In most parts of the world, there is more life within the soil than there is above ground.

These creatures are important because they make life possible for plants. The miracle of plants is that they can take simple nutrients from the soil and air and put them together to make the special, complex chemicals that we need as food.

But plants have their limitations, too. They cannot turn food chemicals back into the simple nutrients that *they* need to grow. This is what the soil creatures do. They are "decomposers," which means that they take the complex chemicals apart and get them ready to be used again by plants.

In other words, they make things rot.

Nothing can decay all by itself. Although we may say, for example, that "a leaf rots," the leaf

Rotten Racers!

Pick two leaves that are just about alike. Place one on a clean saucer. Place the other on a saucer of moist dirt. Cover both leaves with plastic bags. See how they look after a few days, a week, two weeks. Which leaf rots faster? Why?

STEP OUT ON A SOIL SAFARI

You can see some of the world's most exotic animals right in your playground or backyard. Here's all you need:

- A patch of good soil, like a flower bed or garden.
- A sieve or colander to run the soil through. This will help you find the larger animals.
- A jar to put animals in while you look at them.
- A magnifying glass, if you have one, so you can get a close-up view of the small fry.
- A notebook, to draw pictures or

descriptions of the creatures you find.

First, sit and watch the dirt for a while. Who do you see? Can you tell where they're going or what they eat? How might they be helping the plants to grow?

Dig up a handful of dirt and break it apart. Who do you see now? What can you tell about them?

If you want a closer look at the animals you find, try scooping them up gently with a jar or trowel. Remember to put them back where you found them after you've had a peek.

doesn't actually do anything; it just lies there. The action only begins when mold starts to grow on the leaf or a worm crawls out of the soil and takes a bite. Soon, a soil-mite may show up to browse on the mold; a ground beetle catches the worm. It's a hungry world down there; everything is eaten and changed. Even the beetle's droppings may become food for an earthworm as it munches its way through the soil. The earthworm's castings may provide nourishment for other small creatures. And so it goes.

As the material from the leaf is eaten, digested and excreted over and over again, the complex chemicals are gradually broken apart. Soon they are ready to be taken up by plant roots and used to grow more food.

Starring the Soil Creatures!

A good place to see the soil creatures in action, and to admire the results of their work, is in the woods. Crouch down and sweep away the covering of loose leaves. Underneath, you will find a layer of dark, crumbly soil with a pleasant "earthy" smell. This is what becomes of leaves and other plant remains, animal wastes and dead bodies when they have been worked over by the soil creatures for a while. They turn into a kind of rich dirt called "humus."

Topsoil—the few centimeters at the surface where most of the soil creatures live—is made of humus mixed with clay and sand. It is the humus that provides most of the nutrients plants need to grow. At the same time, humus provides food for the soil creatures themselves, including some that assist plants in surprising ways. There are fuzzy little mold-like creatures, for example, that grow

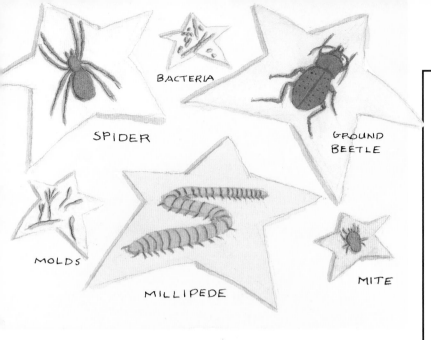

SPIDER
BACTERIA
GROUND BEETLE
MOLDS
MILLIPEDE
MITE

around plant roots and actually help the plants take what they need from the soil. Other creatures produce vitamins that make the plants grow fast.

There are also several kinds of bacteria (simple, bag-like creatures, far smaller than the prick of a pin) that make nutrients for plants. Plants need a chemical called nitrogen, which is everywhere around us in the air. Unfortunately, plants cannot take nitrogen from the air, but—wouldn't you know it?—these bacteria can. They put the nitrogen into a form that will stay in the soil, and then other bacteria change it again and again, until it is just right for plants. Some of these bacteria live in little sacks on the roots of common plants such as peas, beans, lentils, alfalfa and clover. (These plants are called "legumes.")

Amazing, isn't it? And it's all going on right under our toes.

This is the way the Earth prepares the soil for plants. It's a tried and true method that has kept the planet green for millions and millions of years. And it will go on working for us—if we let it.

In the Soup

Scientists have invented a way to grow food without dirt. It is called "hydroponics," or "farming with water," and it is done in specially equipped greenhouses. Instead of soil, plants are given a thin soup of water and nutrients; their roots suck what they need out of this mixture.

Hydroponics works, but it cannot grow the huge quantities of food that five billion people require. For that, we need topsoil.

Feeding Our Friends in the Soil / **21**

BE A HUMAN HUMUS HELPER

Since the soil feeds you, it is only fair that you should feed it, too. Its favorite "food" is humus, or compost. Here's how to cook up a batch.

Step 1: Collect kitchen scraps and yard wastes—egg shells, vegetable rinds, fruit peels, tea leaves, coffee grounds, grass clippings, leaves. You'll need a container in your kitchen to put things in. A plastic ice-cream bucket works well. For fast compost, chop everything into small bits.

Do not put in meat, bones, cheese or fat, which might attract animals to your compost.

Step 2: Make a compost pile. Choose a corner of your garden where you can dump what you've saved. (Some people prefer to make their compost in a special bin, but it's not necessary.) Make your heap in layers, starting with a finger's depth of rich garden soil, well-rotted manure or compost starter from the garden store. This layer will provide enough soil creatures to make the compost work. Then add a layer of kitchen and yard scraps, about twice the height of your hand, and sprinkle a few shovelfuls of soil on top. Then add more scraps, more soil, and so on.

Keep your compost moist, like a squeezed-out sponge, and turn it with a shovel about once a month. You'll have finished compost in six months to a year.

Step 3: Spread the compost on your garden. Then stand back and watch those salads, soups, berry pies and jack-o-lanterns grow!

ON YOUR MARK, GET SET, GROW

Get two large plant pots. Fill one with dirt from a garden or flowerbed. Fill the other with a mixture of dirt and humus. (For humus, use compost from a compost pile, composted manure from a garden store or rotted leaves from the woods.) Plant two tomato seeds in each pot. Water them well when you plant them. As the days pass, give them just enough water to keep the soil moist. Which plants grow better? Which do you have to water most often? Why?

Treating the Soil Like Dirt

Whenever we take food off a farm, we are carrying away nutrients that used to be in the soil. A bag of carrots, for example, contains nutrients that were drawn out of the topsoil by the carrots' roots; a jug of milk contains goodness that was taken up by hay plants and then eaten by a cow.

When we take nutrients away, we have to give something back to the soil to make it rich again. One good way of doing this is to feed the soil creatures—to give them animal wastes or dying plants to eat. For example, we can spread manure or compost on our fields or plant legumes to put nitrogen into the soil. Later, the legumes can be plowed right into the ground and so can the leftover parts of other plants (the leaves and stems that we cannot eat). These all provide food for the soil creatures, which in turn provide nutrients for our next crop of carrots or hay.

But in about the last hundred years, people have invented a simpler way to give nutrients to

Turning Fuel into Food

Growing food is work, and it takes energy. For example, farm trucks and tractors run on energy from gasoline. A great deal of energy is also used to manufacture fertilizers. Nitrogen fertilizer is made out of natural gas, a fuel that we pipe up from deep underground. Natural gas from inside the Earth is non-renewable; when we use it up, we cannot make any more. Nitrogen fertilizer is non-renewable, too. Once we've used it, it will never be there to help people grow food again.

plants. They manufacture fertilizers and spread them on the soil. Factory-made fertilizers contain a few of the nutrients that plants need to grow, usually N (nitrogen), P (phosphorus) and K (potassium); some contain S (sulfur) as well. The numbers on the bag tell you how much of each nutrient the fertilizer contains.

Factory-made fertilizers are extremely valuable. If we feed the soil creatures well and *then* add a sprinkling of fertilizer, we can produce more food than the soil would naturally grow. When the five billion people on Earth have increased to six or eight or ten billion, those extra mouthfuls of food could make us very glad!

POLLUTION IS NO SOLUTION

Factory-made fertilizers can cause pollution. For example, nitrogen fertilizer can hurt the soil by making it sour, or acidic. Plants and soil creatures do not grow well in sour soil. In some regions, the rain is acidic, too, because of pollution from cars, trucks, factories and power plants. This makes the sour-soil problem even worse.

Nitrogen fertilizer can hurt the water if it washes out of the soil into rivers, lakes and wells. In time, the people who drink this polluted water may get very sick.

Nitrogen fertilizer can even hurt the atmosphere. High above the Earth, there is a special layer of air, called ozone, which protects us from bad sunburns and some serious illnesses. Chemicals from fertilizer sometimes float out of the soil and travel all the way up through the atmosphere. Here they "eat up" ozone. If too much ozone is destroyed, plants will get sunburned, too, and stop growing properly. What will happen to us then?

If we keep the soil healthy by feeding the soil creatures, we can use less factory-made fertilizer and cause less damage to the soil, water and air.

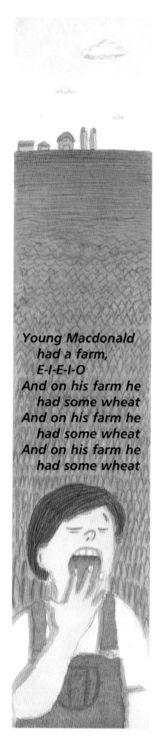

Young Macdonald had a farm, E-I-E-I-O And on his farm he had some wheat And on his farm he had some wheat And on his farm he had some wheat

There is a small but growing group of "alternative" farmers who care for their land by looking after the soil creatures first and then adding a little bit of fertilizer. Other farmers grow food "organically," which means that they have learned to feed their soil without factory-made fertilizers.

But there are still many straight-thinkers who believe that fussing over the soil creatures is a waste of money and time. Planting legumes is too much work, they say, and manure is hard to find because modern farms are very specialized. Farmers who grow only corn, for example, do not have chickens, cows or pigs to give them manure. And, anyway, a farmer's job is to produce food, right? Not to worry about a bunch of bugs and microbes in the dirt. So just pour on the factory-made fertilizer and watch the crops grow!

This is how much of our food is grown. But there are problems with doing this, and some day soon there will be big problems unless we change our ways.

Young Macdonald Is a Bore

Remember "Old Macdonald," with his baa-baa here and moo-moo there and cluck-cluck somewhere else? Farms were actually like that not so long ago. Ask your parents or grandparents. They'll probably be able to tell you about farms they knew when they were kids, where you could ride horses, feed ducks, rustle through wheat fields, stuff yourself with raspberries or hunt for chicken eggs.

But farms are different now. Somebody got the idea that farmers could grow more food if they specialized, like factories do, and grew only one crop—just corn, just wheat, just onions. So now huge areas are planted to a single plant; year after year after year, the fields look the same. This is called "monoculture." Monoculture is boring and, worse, it's hard on the soil. Nature grows all sorts of different plants together, and that's what the soil likes best.

Growing animals for meat, milk and eggs has been specialized, too. Chickens, for example, are raised—thousands, even hundreds of thousands at a time—in tiny wire cells, stacked wall to wall and ceiling to floor. In their entire lives, these chickens never see the sun, catch a bug or breathe fresh air; they can hardly stretch their wings. Cows that are to be used for meat are fattened in fenced-in areas called feedlots, where they are crowded

together by the hundreds or thousands. Because they live in such unhealthy conditions, many food animals have to be given medicine all the time to keep them from getting sick.

The way we raise our animals is also bad for the soil. In the not-so-old days, when most farmers had livestock *and* crops, manure from the animals could easily be spread on the farm's own fields. But today the people who have the manure don't grow any crops. The people who grow the crops don't have any manure. It is usually too expensive to truck the stuff around. The feedlots have so much manure they don't know what to do, and the crop-growers' soils are starved.

MEATY MATTERS

- In Sweden people grew so concerned about the way farm animals were being treated that the government passed a new law. It says that pigs cannot be kept in bare cages anymore. Instead, they must be free to roam around and to wallow in the mud. They must be given straw to lie down on. How do farm animals live in your country? Are there laws to protect them? How could you or your class find out?
- The next time you go shopping, see if you can find "natural" or

"range-fed" meats at your grocery or health-food store. These labels mean that the animals were well cared for, did not have to be dosed with medicines and were allowed to move around.

Check the price as well. "Natural" meat is often a little more expensive than the regular kind, which may sound like bad news. But doctors say that many people in rich countries, like ours, eat too much meat, especially beef and pork. This is one reason so many of us die of cancer, heart attacks and strokes. If beef and pork cost a little more, maybe we will eat less of them and more of other high-protein foods such as chicken, fish, peas, beans and lentils. The bad news about "natural" meat may be good news after all.

Hungry for Humus

When the soil creatures are not given manure and dying plants, they are not able to produce very much humus. Losing humus hurts the soil in several ways. Humus-rich soils are "fluffy" and spongy, so they can hold air and moisture around the plant roots; this helps crops grow well. But starved soils cake and dry out, so crops that grow in them wither quickly when there's not much rain. Humus also makes the soil sticky, so that the particles cling to each other and are held in place. But without humus, the soil turns to dust and is readily swept off by wind, snowmelt and rain. This is called "erosion." In many parts of the world, topsoil is being worn away twice as fast as it is being produced. Yet without topsoil to hold nutrients and water around the plant roots, we cannot grow food.

In some cities, kitchen and yard wastes are collected from everyone and composted all together. The compost is used in nearby parks, gardens and farms.

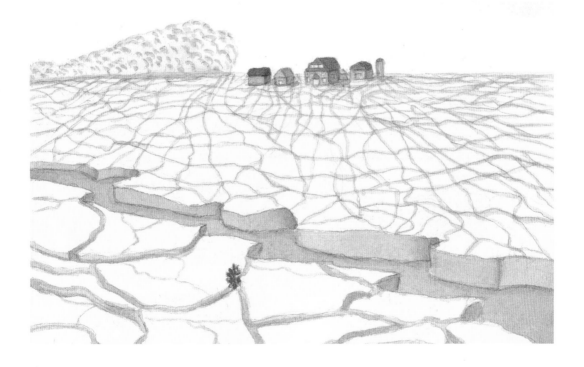

Feeding Our Friends in the Soil / **29**

Farmers in the United States now use twice as much nitrogen fertilizer as they did twenty years ago. Farmers on the Canadian prairies use six times more.

The next time you walk in the woods, think about the soil. What does the Earth do to care for it? How can you use these ideas in your garden?

Soils that lose humus also lose their fertility, their natural ability to make plants grow. Year by year, we have to use more and more fertilizer to get the food we need.

To make matters even worse, fertilizers are expensive. So are seed, farm equipment, gasoline and the chemicals some farmers use to kill insects and weeds. But the prices that farmers get for their crops and livestock are often quite low (far less than we pay to buy the same food at the grocery store). People sometimes call this the "cost-price squeeze."

Squeezed between big bills and small incomes, farmers are forced to grow and sell as much as they possibly can. Every last clod of dirt—even soils that are too sandy or steep for growing food— must be made to produce. So marshes and ponds, which could have helped the soil to hold water, are drained and plowed. (Where do the ducks go then?) Stands of trees are chopped and burned to make way for crops. (Now where will the butter-flies lay their eggs and the songbirds build their nests?)

By cultivating every last scrap of land, some farmers are able to grow enough to pay their bills and stay in business for another year. But all around us, the future—the topsoil—is drying up and blowing off faster than ever; it is washing in great muddy streams into the rivers and seas. Away goes the last of the humus; soon only sand will be left. This is called "desertification," and it is happening in many parts of the Earth. Once land has been turned to desert, it takes years of work and piles of cash to make it grow food again.

Thinking straight about the soil takes us straight into difficulty.

Areas that are already desert.

Areas that will likely become desert unless we treat them with care.

FARMER, SPARE THAT TREE!

People all over the world have been clearing away woodlands for many centuries. There didn't seem to be much choice. How could we have farms with forests everywhere? So axe them, burn them, get them out of there.

We now know that this loss is dangerous. Trees, it turns out, are very important creatures. For one thing, they help prevent the climate of the Earth from warming up because of the Greenhouse Effect. For another, they protect the soil. They hold it with their roots and keep it from wearing away; they feed it with their fallen leaves; they branch out and shelter it from the drying sun.

In Brazil and other tropical

BRAZIL

countries, huge areas of jungle are still being bulldozed and burned to make room for ranches and farms. Almost as soon as the land is stripped of trees the soil starts to die. At most it can grow food for six or seven years. But if the trees were left in place, they would protect the growing power of the soil. They would also produce foods such as nuts and fruits, which people would be able to gather and eat for many centuries.

All over the world—in Brazil, Canada, Nigeria, Kenya, China, the Philippines—scientists and farmers are learning how trees can be used to help us grow food. One common method is to plant trees in bands or rows, with room for crops in between. Within this shelter, the crops produce more than they would otherwise, and the trees provide fruits, firewood, lumber and food for animals. Some of the trees even add nitrogen to the soil, the same way legumes do.

SOIL WORDS

"Alternative" farm: A farm where the soil is fed dying plants, legumes and manure to keep it healthy, and where factory-made fertilizer is also used.

Compost: Rotted plants and animal wastes that people prepare to use on their gardens and farms. Compost is a kind of humus and is very good for the soil.

Decomposers: Creatures in the soil that make things rot. Decomposers take the complicated chemicals in dead plants and animal droppings and turn them into simple nutrients that plants need to grow.

Desertification: Turning good soil into sandy desert. Land may turn to desert if it is cultivated too much and starved for humus, or if it is grazed too much by too many goats or cows.

Erosion: Loss of topsoil when it is swept away by wind or water.

Fertility: The ability of soil to make plants grow.

Fertilizer: Something that is put on soil to provide the nutrients plants need to grow. Animal manure is called an "organic" fertilizer. Factory-made fertilizers are sometimes called "chemical" fertilizers.

Greenhouse Effect: The warming of the climate of the Earth caused by exhaust from cars, trucks and factories. Trees help prevent this change by making the atmosphere healthy again.

Humus: The part of the topsoil that comes from rotted plants, animal bodies and animal wastes.

Hydroponics: Growing plants in a mixture of water and nutrients, without soil.

Legumes: Certain plants, such as peas, beans and alfalfa, which make the soil richer just by growing in it.

Monoculture: Growing one crop over large areas, year after year. ("Mono" means "one.")

Nitrogen: A chemical that plants need in order to grow.

"Organic" farm: A farm where food is grown without factory-made fertilizers or other farm chemicals. "Organic" farmers rely mainly on legumes and manure to enrich their soil.

Topsoil: The thin, top layer of soil that supplies plants with most of the nutrients they need to grow. Topsoil is being lost fast in many parts of the world.

FIND THE (DIRTY) DIFFERENCES

Here are two farms. On one of them, the soil is being neglected. On the other, it is well cared for. Which is which? How is the soil being protected on the well-run farm? Which farm will be able to grow more food when you're a grandparent?

See page 35 for answers.

Which farm would lose more food to weed and insect "pests"? Turn to page 47 if you need a clue.

How to Grow Healthy Soil

So what are we going to do? If we leave the soil creatures out of our thinking, the soil dies. We gradually lose our ability to grow food. Happily, the answer is clear. It is time to think in round-about ways and work with the Earth again. We must care for the living soil.

A farm is not a wilderness, and we cannot look after the soil exactly as the Earth would. But if we think about the way nutrients move through the soil, to plants and animals and then back to the soil again, we can imitate the way the Earth works.

- The first rule for a healthy soil is to feed the soil creatures. If we feed them, they will provide nutrients for our crops.
- The second rule is to keep the soil covered as much as possible with growing plants or dead leaves and stems. This will make life comfortable for the creatures in the soil and help to keep the soil from blowing or washing away.
- The third rule is to dig and disturb the soil as little as we can. The soil lies in layers, with the soil creatures and their humus-rich earth on top. When we turn the soil over, the topsoil ends up on the bottom, which is not where it belongs!

Even when the topsoil is left on top, it should not be dug or tilled too much. When topsoil is cultivated, the soil creatures get extra oxygen and become more active and hungrier than usual. They may eat up everything that we feed them, plus the humus that is already in the soil, and leave us worse off than we were before.

- The fourth rule is to love variety. When different plants grow on the same land, together or in different years, the soil gets healthier. (We know this is true, though we don't always know quite why.) So we shouldn't seed the same crop over large areas year after year. Instead, we can grow many kinds of plants, including soil-feeding legumes, and keep animals, too. It's easier to keep the soil rich if there's animal manure to put on it. We can also plant trees to protect the soil from being swept away by the wind and rain.

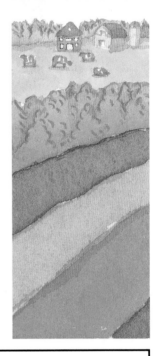

If we follow these rules, and others we will someday learn from observing the Earth, our farms will grow strong, healthy soil—soil that is able to feed you, your kids (when you have them) and your great-great-grandchildren, too.

ANSWERS TO "FIND THE (DIRTY) DIFFERENCES"
The farm on the right treats its soil better than the one on the left. It will probably be able to grow more food when you're a grandparent. Here are some of the differences you may have noticed:
- The trees on the well-run farm protect the soil from erosion.
- Crops are planted in strips so that several different kinds can be grown together. The short one is a legume, which puts nitrogen into the soil.

- Cattle are kept for meat or milk and for manure. The manure is spread on the soil to feed the soil creatures.
- The steep hillside is used as pasture. The grass prevents the soil from being washed away.
- Stubble (straw) is left on the field to protect the soil, not burned.
- The tractor is small so that it doesn't pack the soil down too badly.
- A special "chisel" plow is used so that the soil won't be badly disturbed when it is cultivated.

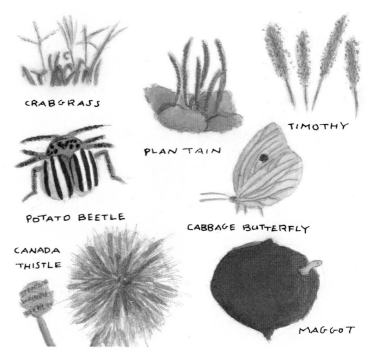

PESTS

BULLY

MATH TEACHER

OLDER SISTER

DANDELION

CATERPILLAR

CRABGRASS

PLANTAIN

TIMOTHY

POTATO BEETLE

CABBAGE BUTTERFLY

CANADA THISTLE

MAGGOT

CHAPTER 3
Making Peace With "Pests"

When we're talking about food, the word "pest" has a special meaning. It gets serious. "Pests" are weeds, insects and other creatures that take food out of our mouths. They reduce the amount of food that gets to the grocery store.

Consider weeds, for example. When weeds take over a garden or farm, they soak up water and nutrients from the soil—goodness that we want to go into our food plants instead. If the weeds outgrow the crops, they even grab most of the sunshine, while our food plants struggle on, stunted and shriveled in their shade.

Or think about insects. Soft green caterpillars that munch on young cabbage plants. Maggots that burrow into radish roots and turn them to mush. Cities of aphids that feast on hay crops or lettuce plants.

Mountains of food are lost each year to weeds, worms, insects, fruit-eating birds, mice and rats. Something has to be done about it, and fast!

But before we get too heated up, let's stop for a minute and think this through again. Weeds are simply plants that are growing in the wrong place or that we don't know how to use. There's nothing evil about them. They just happen to be in our way at the moment. In the future, who knows? Someone may someday take a new look at the plants that we call weeds and decide that they'd make good crops. After all, the plants we now grow for food were wild once, and there's no law to say people have to go on eating the same things forever.

Or what if weeds could some day help us to make new food-plants in the laboratory. Scientists are now learning to take characteristics from one kind of plant and put them into other kinds. (Can they give chocolate flavor to strawberries? Legume roots to wheat?) It is a sad fact, for example, that the soil in many parts of the world is becoming salty. This is happening because people are watering, or irrigating, the land in order to grow food. (When the extra water seeps down deep into the soil, salts from underground dissolve and float up into the topsoil.) Many of our present food crops do not grow well on salty ground, but some weeds can. Scientists may soon be able to take this characteristic—the ability to grow on salty ground—out of the weeds and put it into our food plants.

Weeds can be a nuisance, but they are also a rich resource.

Spy on a Spider
Spiders help put food on your plate. They eat the insects that try to eat your food before it gets to you. Prove it for yourself by watching the spiders in your garden or park. What do they eat? How do they catch their food? Do they all weave webs? How many types can you find? (Be sure to check in flowers and under rocks—look sharp for the camouflage experts!) Have you ever seen one that runs sideways like a crab?

*Making Peace with "Pests" / **37***

The bugs that look to us like pests
May be what baby birds like best.

Weeds also help us in another, round-about way by providing food and shelter for many creatures, including insects and spiders. What good does this do us? We're inclined to think that insects and spiders are ugly—google-eyed, with too many legs—and probably bad. But, in fact, insects and spiders help to keep the Earth beautiful and interesting. For example, did you know that they serve as "baby food" for all songbirds? Without insects and spiders, there would be very few birds. There would be no bird-eating creatures such as foxes and falcons.

Some insects and most spiders also help us to grow food for ourselves. They do this by eating insect "pests," the ones that hurt our crops. Of the thousands of different kinds of insects in the world, very few (perhaps 1 in 100) eat our food plants. All the rest help us either directly, by eating the harmful bugs, or indirectly, by providing food for the birds and animals with which we share the Earth.

Whatever we do to control farm "pests," we had better be smart about it!

Knock 'em Dead!

Straight-thinkers do not spend a lot of time wondering about the importance of weeds or insects. They just want to get rid of them. For the past fifty years, their favorite way of dealing with "pests" has been to use special poisons, which are called "pesticides." Much of what we eat—grapes, strawberries, lettuce, cornflakes, bread—is grown with the help of pesticides.

The very first pesticides were invented by plants. For example, the roots of a grass called rye (the grain from which rye bread is made) produce

a chemical that keeps other plants from growing nearby. It is a natural herbicide. Flowers such as chrysanthemums and marigolds contain natural insecticides. These chemicals cannot do any great harm to the Earth when they are held inside plants. But people have learned to take the poisons out of the plants and spread them all over their crops to kill insects and weeds. These products are sometimes sold as natural or "organic" pesticides.

But most of the pesticides in use today do not occur naturally on Earth; they are invented in laboratories and made in factories. You will find them in bottles, cans and boxes at the garden shop. The skull-and-crossbones on the package tells you that the pesticide is poison; the name on the label tells you what it is meant to kill. "Herbicides," or weed-killers, for example, are made to kill certain types of plants; "insecticides" are made to kill . . . guess what!

Pesticides are widely used because they work fast. They are one of the tools that we can use as we try to keep everyone fed, a kind of secret weapon to help us out of real emergencies. But

In the United States alone, more than 200 million kilograms (440 million pounds) of pesticide are used to grow food each year.

In the time it takes for an orange to grow, the fruit may be sprayed with pesticides ten to twenty times.

Food should not pass your inspection If it's poisoned to perfection.

they should not be used every day, on every farm, to grow our food. Both "organic" and factory-made pesticides can be dangerous.

Problems with Pesticides

The worst thing about pesticides is that they often work too well. They do not know when to stop killing. A herbicide that is sprayed on a field to get the weeds does not know that it is supposed to stop killing if it trickles into a marsh. When marsh plants die, the ducks may go hungry. Next year and the next and the next, there are likely to be fewer and fewer ducks.

Insect poisons cannot tell the difference between a bug that is biting into one of our precious tomatoes and a spider that is doing its best to catch the tomato bug. Boom! Cough! Both are dead, along with the other six- and eight-legged creatures in the neighborhood. What happens to the baby birds then?

Some pesticides are put on the land in the form of pellets, which look like fine gravel or seeds. When wild birds eat the pellets, they are often

---

"PERFECT" PRODUCE?

Here are two apples.

The one on the left was sprayed with pesticides. It looks picture perfect because any insects that tried

to bite it were poisoned to death. So were any other insects or spiders that happened to be in the neighborhood. Many wild animals and birds went hungry as a result.

The apple on the right was grown in an orchard where pesticides were not used. Nothing was poisoned to grow this fruit. It has a little mark on it because an insect took a bite.

Which apple is perfect for you?

killed. In the corn-growing regions of Ontario, Canada, as many as 200,000 birds may die this way each year.

Using pesticides to control weeds and insects is like dropping a bomb on a city in order to stop a few thieves. Too many innocent bystanders end up dead.

Do not get into a panic. Shop for "Certified Organic."

HOLD THE PESTICIDE!

If you do not want to eat pesticides with your food, here are some things you can do.

- Scrub and peel fruits and vegetables. Most of the pesticide residues are on or near the surface of the food, where they can be removed.

- Shop for food that is marked "Certified Organic." This label tells you two things. "Organic" means that no factory-made pesticides were used. "Certified" means that the farm has been inspected, so you don't have to take the grower's word for it. (To become certified, a farmer must also take very good care of the soil.) If you cannot get food that is certified organic, look for "organic" food instead. It is probably okay, but you cannot be as sure.

- If you cannot get "organic" food, talk to the store manager. If more people ask, more stores will carry it and the price will come down. There are already chains of grocery stores in Britain, California and other places that sell organic produce.

- Shop at the local farmers' market. Get to know the people who grow your food. Talk to them about "pests" and pesticides. Buy from someone who manages "pests" wisely. (Ask them how they care for the soil, too.)

Do Pesticides Make People Sick?

Although people look very different from beetles and dandelions, we are more like them than we seem to be. Many of the chemicals that occur naturally in our bodies are almost the same as those that occur inside insects and weeds. Pesticides work because they affect some of these chemicals. If pesticides kill "pests," do they hurt us, too?

The answer is a frustrating "yes," "no" and "maybe so." Yes, most pesticides can be harmful, especially to the people who handle them. This includes many of the people who grow our food. The danger is especially great when someone forgets to follow all the safety rules. Thousands of people are poisoned each year, mostly in poorer countries, because they are not trained or equipped to use pesticides safely.

Anyone who uses weed- or bug-killer should read the instructions on the package and follow them *exactly*. Otherwise they may get sick or even die. It is also important to dispose of the empty containers as Hazardous Waste. They should never be left lying around or thrown in the garbage.

But what about people who do not use pesticides? Are we in danger, too? Many experts say that the answer is "no." For one thing, most present-day pesticides are made to decompose in the soil—they usually break down quite quickly into chemicals that are not thought to be dangerous. They do not go on being poisonous forever and should not collect in our bodies or elsewhere on Earth, the way DDT did.

All the same, some pesticides do get into our food—especially into vegetables and fruits—in their original, poisonous state. They are present in very small amounts. Many experts believe that

THE DDT DISASTER

When the first pesticides were invented, everyone got very excited. The scientist who developed DDT, a powerful insecticide, was given the Nobel Prize. People thought that the war against hunger and disease had been won, because insects that harmed people in any way could now be killed.

For the first twenty years or so, everything seemed to be fine. Then something terrible started to happen. Birds like eagles, osprey and peregrine falcons began to vanish in many parts of the world.

The main problem turned out to be DDT, which was building up in the birds' food. The wonder pesticide was not so wonderful after all. DDT was banned in North America and Europe around 1970, and the eagles and other birds began to recover, with a great deal of very expensive help from humankind.

Meanwhile, hundreds of new pesticides have been invented and put

into use. We know that they are not likely to cause exactly the same problems as DDT did, but we cannot tell what unexpected trouble they may bring. Are we in for another nasty surprise after twenty years?

Tweet! Scientists in Denmark have proven that "organic" farms, where pesticides are not used, have more birds on them than other farms do.

these tiny traces, or "residues," are safe. After all, there are many natural poisons in our food, which our bodies know how to change into harmless chemicals. We can also deal with trace amounts of pesticides, they say.

What's more, the law says that pesticides must be tested carefully before they can be sold. As part of this research, each pesticide is fed to laboratory mice or rats. Researchers check to see if the animals get cancer or other sicknesses. Are their babies all right? If there are problems, how much poison can they handle before they get sick? Based on these studies, scientists decide how much pesticide an adult person can safely eat. Then they divide this amount by 100, just to be extra sure. This is the most that is allowed in our food.

Workers in the department of health constantly check samples of food to see how much pesticide they contain. They almost never find anything that breaks the rules. They say our food is very safe.

But other people are not reassured. They have a lot of questions and very few answers. Here are some of the things they would like to know.

- Do tests carried out on animals really tell us how pesticides affect people?
- The amount of pesticide that is allowed in our food is set for adults. Yet babies and children cannot handle poisons as well as grown-ups can; neither can old folks. Are the "safe" levels safe for them?
- In many parts of Europe and North America, pesticides have trickled into the wells, rivers and lakes where our drinking water comes from. If we get pesticides in our food *and* in our water,

44 / *Get Growing*

are we still under the "safe" levels?
- Will our bodies get so worn out dealing with all the extra poisons that we start to get sick more easily? (This may already be happening to some people.)
- What happens when traces of several pesticides meet in our bodies at once? Almost no one has studied this.

- What will happen in the long run, over a few hundred years? Are there problems we haven't noticed yet? Will we find out when it is too late, when all we are able to do is try to clean up the mess?
- If pesticides *are* hurting people in ways we don't understand, what might they be doing to the insects, plants, animals and birds?

I think the "maybe's" are right. There is too much we still don't know. By using huge amounts of pesticides, we are conducting a reckless experiment on ourselves, our grandchildren and the rest of the living world. We do not have to take this risk.

THESE PESTICIDES ARE ALIVE!

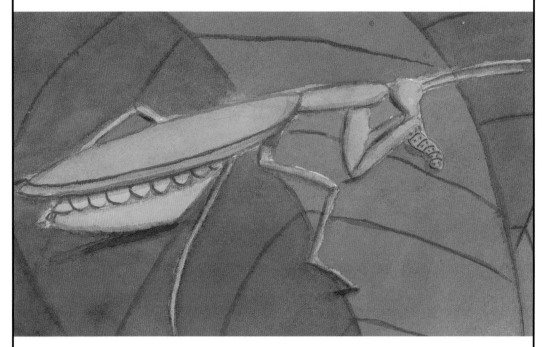

Living creatures can sometimes be used as pesticides. They are safer than chemical pesticides because they are specific. They are chosen for use because they can only harm the "pest" itself.

Here's how they work. Farmers in Canada had problems with a weed, a kind of thistle. So scientists started studying all the insects that eat thistle seeds. They finally found one that eats only the seeds of that particular kind of thistle, nothing else. They then got permission from the government to raise a lot of these insects and give them to farmers. The farmers turned the insects loose and soon, munch, munch, the thistle was under control.

In Africa, millions of people depend on a root crop called cassava. This plant originally grew in South America and was carried across the ocean about four hundred years ago. Although nobody noticed it at the time, mealybugs that like to eat cassava plants made the journey, too. But the insects that naturally control these "pests" were left back in Brazil. Scientists have now found a kind of South American wasp that kills these mealybugs and does not harm any other insects in Africa. This wasp is being used to protect cassava crops in eighteen countries. This method of dealing with pests is called "biological control."

No Problem!

We must control insects and weeds; otherwise we have no hope of feeding the five billion people on Earth. But we do not have to use pesticides as our first and only defense. If we think and work with the round-about ways of the Earth, many "pest" problems can be cured without poisons. In fact, many of the problems we struggle with now don't have to be problems at all.

- The first rule for preventing "pest" problems is to care for the soil. If our crops are planted in healthy soil, they will be healthy, too. No weeds will be able to crowd them out. And if insects browse them down, the healthy food plants will just grow back. The "pests" won't have a chance to cause any real harm.
- The second rule is to choose our crops with care. Scientists have developed many different varieties of our favorite food plants, such as lettuce, tomatoes and corn. (If you look in a seed catalogue from a garden store, you'll find them listed there.) Some of these varieties taste horrible to bugs, because they contain natural insecticides. Some of them grow very fast and can crowd out weeds. If our food plants can fight back for themselves, they don't need our help. We can just relax and get ready to eat them for lunch!

Super "Pests"

When a field is sprayed with pesticide, many of the "pests" immediately die. But there are always some that survive. These are individuals that are especially hard to poison. When these hardy survivors reproduce, their offspring are likely to be super-tough, as well. Soon most of the "pests" in the area are the hard-to-poison sort, which the pesticide cannot kill. Hundreds of kinds of insects and weeds are now more difficult to control because they have been made stronger through the use of pesticides.

PEST WORDS

Biological control: A way of fighting "pests" by using their natural enemies, such as predators, parasites and sicknesses.

Cancer: A serious illness that may be caused by some pesticides and other harmful chemicals.

Certified Organic: A label that is used to mark food that is known to have been grown without pesticides or factory-made fertilizer.

Crop rotation: Planting a field to different crops from year to year.

DDT: One of the first insecticides. It caused certain birds to stop having young.

Herbicides: Chemicals that kill plants.

Insecticides: Chemicals that kill insects.

Integrated Pest Management: A step-by-step method of controlling "pests" that often helps to reduce the amount of pesticide used.

Mulching: Covering the ground to keep weeds from growing. Grass clippings, wood chips and plastic can all be used for mulching.

Pests: Living things that are a nuisance to people.

Pesticides: Chemicals that are made to kill insects, weeds and other "pests" that reduce the amount of food we can grow. Some people think they should be called "biocides," or life-killers, because they do not kill only "pests."

Residues: Tiny amounts of pesticide that get into our food.

• The third rule is to raise many different kinds of plants and animals. (This is doubly good because it helps the soil, too.) Many pest problems happen because our farms are all-one-thing. Every crop has certain weeds and insects that like to live with it; these "pests" leave their seeds and eggs in the soil each fall. If the same crop is planted the following spring, the "pests" are waiting there, ready to make trouble again.

But if the field is planted to a different crop, the "pests" will become uncomfortable and die away. Planting an area to different crops from year to year is called "crop rotation."
- The fourth rule is to love wildness. Provide living spaces for all kinds of insects and birds. Plant bushes and trees. Save roadsides and wetlands. Conserve wild places. If we look after the birds

PUTTING WEEDS TO WORK

Here are four ways to use the weeds in your garden or park. Can you think of four more?
- Enjoy them. Smell them. Draw them. Wear them in your hair.
- Eat them. Lamb's quarters and tender spring dandelion leaves are great in salads. (Only pick them in places where you know that no one has been using weed-killer.)
- Study them. Get to know them by name. See what kinds of insects

live in them. Are these insects useful in your garden?
- Learn from them. See what they tell you about your soil. Wild daisies, for example, grow where the soil is poor. They say, "Put on more compost." Chickweed, on the other hand, means the soil is rich. What kinds of soil do other weeds like? How can you use what they tell you?

and animals that eat weed seeds and insect "pests," they will help us grow food. We won't even have to ask.

Many "organic" farmers have been following these rules for years. They are now being joined by "alternative" farmers, who use a step-by-step approach called Integrated Pest Management. First, alternative farmers follow the four rules for preventing "pest" problems. Second, they check their crops often and learn to tell when the weeds or bugs are starting to do real harm. Then they

DOWN ON ROUND-ABOUT ROAD

The gardeners on Round-About Road use safe methods to outsmart "pests." How do they do it? See how many ways you can find.

See page 52 for answers.

SEED CATALOGUE

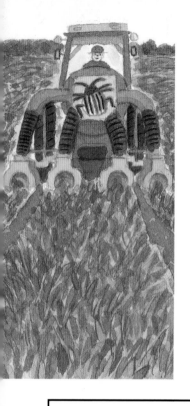

look for safe ways to remove the "pests." (For example, they may plow up weeds or use biological controls. Some strawberry growers have special vacuum cleaners that suck insects off the plants.) Fourth, if there is no other choice, they use a chemical pesticide, taking time to choose the one that will cause the least harm.

By working in this way, farmers all around the world—in Canada, California, Sweden, Indonesia and elsewhere—have been able to grow excellent crops using little or no pesticide. What's more, their soil is healthy, and their farms are alive with butterflies, bees, bunnies, squirrels, ducks and singing birds. When we make mistakes in the way we grow our food, the harm often carries on, causing problems we didn't expect. But when we get things right, the good is passed along, too, and brings us surprising benefits.

We are not alone. If we think and work with the living Earth, it will help us grow our food. The

---

ANSWERS TO "DOWN ON ROUND-ABOUT ROAD"
- They make compost and spread it on their gardens, so their plants will be healthy and able to resist weeds and insects.
- They read seed catalogues to find out which varieties of plants are bothered the least by insects and weeds.
- They plant trees and put up bird houses to attract insect-eating birds.
- They let part of the yard go wild to attract spiders and insect-eating insects. These predators will help control "pests."
- They put grass clippings down between the rows to keep weeds from growing. This is called mulching.
- They grow many different kinds of crops. They do not grow the same crop in the same place every year.
- They take advantage of "companion planting." For example, putting chrysanthemums around strawberries helps to keep the fruit safe. Bugs hate those flowers and stay away. In the same way, peppermint plants protect cabbages.
- They plant geraniums to attract certain beetles away from the vegetables. The geraniums are used as a "trap" crop. The insects may chew on the flowers, but the food plants will be safe.

birds, insects, animals, plants, soil, air, sunshine and rain will help us if we give them a chance. We do not have to manage by ourselves—in fact, we can't.

GOVERNING THE GOVERNMENT

In some countries, the government makes it hard for farmers to grow food in better ways. For example, some governments give farmers extra money if they plant large areas to certain crops, such as wheat and corn. (This comes from the old idea that monocultures are the best way to grow food.) Farmers who grow many different crops, or who plant some of their land to trees, do not get the extra cash. As a result, some farmers say they cannot afford to care for their soil or control "pests" in Earth-friendly ways.

Talk to people at the farmers' market or to other farmers you know. Invite one of them to speak to your club or class. Find out if your government makes it hard for them to change. If it does, don't fret. Do something! Write to the leader of the government. Design a poster. Make up a song. Publish a pamphlet. Tell your friends. Speak out!

Governments work for us and spend our money. If enough of us say what we want, the government has to change its mind.

Yes We Can!

Picture yourself at the table again, surrounded by piles of food—pots, pans, pitchers and plates of beautiful, beckoning food. Chocolate milk, cookies and carrot sticks. Candy bars, donuts and fizzy drinks. But now you know that this food may have been grown in ways that hurt the Earth. It may have damaged the soil, water and air; it may have killed plants, insects, animals and birds. In the long run, it may have made the Earth a hungrier place to live. But what can you, or anyone, do about it?

When we are faced by a big problem, like the way we grow our food, we want to fix it fast. A big problem should have a big answer, we think—one

Bit by bit
And bite by bite,
We can help
To set things right.

54 / *Get Growing*

big change that will make everything okay. When we can't find the big answer, we feel helpless and confused. We think we can't do anything at all.

But we are wrong about this. A big problem usually does not have one big answer. Instead, it has many, many small answers—dozens of little steps that gradually take us where we have to go. All over the world, people are taking these tiny steps. They are learning to think in round-about ways like the Earth; they are studying the soil, insects, weeds and birds. They are starting gardens, making compost and choosing their food with care, just like you.

By working together, we can care for the living Earth. We can and we must, starting now.

Index